TARGE

TARGET SETTING

by Ian Lawson

The Industrial Society

First published 1966 by
The Industrial Society
Robert Hyde House
48 Bryanston Square
London W1H 7LN
Telephone: 071-262 2401

Second edition 1987
Third edition 1989
© The Industrial Society, 1966, 1987, 1989
Reprinted 1989, 1990

ISBN 0 85290 416 9

British Library Cataloguing in Publication Data
Lawson, Ian
    Target Setting—3rd ed.
    1. Business firms. Planning
    I. Title   II. Industrial Society   III. Series
    658.4'012

Typeset by by Columns of Reading
Printed and bound in Great Britain by Belmont Press, Northampton

CONTENTS

FOREWORD

Whatever the discipline or level of management, the responsibilities of a manager are many and various. It is their job to produce results with essentially just two resources—people and time.

To maximise the potential of both, most managers need some reminders and basic guidelines to help them.

The Notes for Managers series provides succinct yet comprehensive coverage of key management issues and skills. The short time it takes to read each title will pay dividends in terms of utilising one of those key resources—people.

One of the most important actions of a manager is to provide a clear sense of direction for each person in the team. Setting targets after consultation is one way of achieving this.

This booklet is designed to make a series of practical suggestions as to how target setting can be operated by busy managers, regardless of whether or not it fits within a formal appraisal scheme.

ALISTAIR GRAHAM
Director, The Industrial Society

I

TARGET SETTING

INTRODUCTION

For an organisation to be successful, it must recognise that its most important resource and also its greatest variable will always be its people. The problem is not that organisations exploit their people, but that they do not exploit fully the opportunities to use and develop their employees' skills and talents. Target setting will help managers to increase the effectiveness of their people. It can be adopted at any level in an organisation regardless of whether or not a formal appraisal system is in operation.

1

WHAT ARE TARGETS?

Targets are priorities or special tasks which need to be achieved in addition to the routine work. They relate specifically to an individual and are about changes and development. They may be intended to improve performance, to redress a drop in performance, or to develop a trainee to the required level.

Targets are about short-term shifts in performance, whereas standards are continuing yardsticks. This can be shown as in Figure 1.

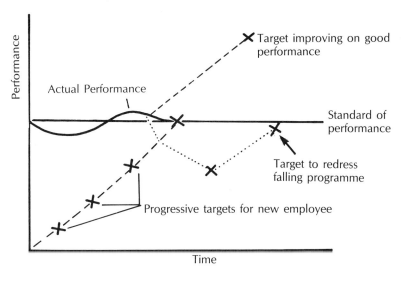

Fig. 1. Relationship of performance to targets over a period of time

2

WHY SET TARGETS?

Targets are set to:

- get results
- improve people's performance
- develop skills, ability and knowledge
- provide a challenge and sense of achievement.

If people are to contribute effectively to the organisation they need to know the answers to certain questions.

- Who is my boss?
- What is my job?
- What is the standard expected of me?
- How am I doing?
- Where do I go from here and how do I get there?

Target setting helps to answer the question 'How am I doing?' and provides a means to address 'Where do I go from here?' and 'How do I get there?'

In order to be effective, target setting requires a drill by which both individual and manager regularly review performance and set new targets. Moreover, clarity of structure within the organisation is helpful as ambiguous structures can produce contradictory targets from two or more bosses. An overall understanding of acceptable standards of performance will also help to provide the baseline for target setting.

3

MANAGEMENT STRUCTURE

It is vital that people are clear about who their boss is and that their immediate boss should be the one who sets targets for them.

For a manager to be able to devote the required attention to a team, experience suggests that there should be no more than 15 direct subordinates. In order to avoid the danger of complexity and concerns over status it is preferable to use departmental accountability charts rather than the conventional structure charts of an organisation.

Dotted lines of accountability may still exist providing one person has the final say and is responsible for the subordinate's performance. In jobs where continually changing projects make this appear impractical, it is important to appoint one manager who is responsible for continuity in the job holder's development programme and for co-ordinating the work done for a series of project managers.

With the first line manager setting targets, a stronger working relationship will be built up and more realistic targets will be set and monitored. Installation of target setting can do as much to make managers accept the responsibility of their people's performance as it can to improve the individual (see Fig. 2.)

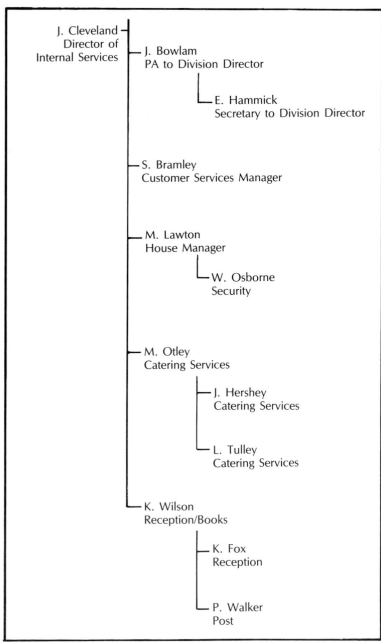

Fig. 2. Example of an accountability chart

4

ESTABLISHING JOB
RESPONSIBILITIES

The next step is for the employee and line manager to establish what contribution the employee is expected to make and how they will measure success.

Traditionally, this has been done by means of a job description, but recently job descriptions have fallen into disrepute for being too complicated and inflexible, and for failing to reflect the actual work done. For a job description to be effective, therefore, it must be updated regularly with the emphasis on what is to be achieved rather than the duties that have to be performed.

People need to know the overall aims of the organisation and department, and, more specifically, the areas to which they will contribute. These are often called key result areas and cover fairly broad headings such as stock, sales, supervision, internal communication, external communication, administration, training and development. They are not a comprehensive list of duties, and it is unlikely that there will be more than six to eight of them. Key result areas will, effectively, state the objectives of the job. Standards of performance will need to be added or incorporated in order for the objectives to express expectations clearly.

Targets are set throughout the year. Key result areas should be set separately by the job holder and the line manager before the two discuss them. This will immediately highlight any discrepancies between their expectations of the job.

5

STANDARDS OF
PERFORMANCE

When key result areas have been identified, standards of performance need to be drawn up. Whereas targets are specific to an individual and tend to be short-term, performance standards relate to the job or position and are longer-term. They act as yardsticks for judging acceptable performance and help job holders to understand what is expected of them. Standards must be objective. Thus, they will either be measurable or recognisable (by adherence to a previously agreed system, for instance).

If no standards are set, it is difficult for job holders to know how they are doing. It is important that both job holder and manager have the same understanding of what standards are expected in order to avoid major disagreements about performance or what targets should be set.

Standards should cover quality as well as quantity, and should emphasise what result the job holder should achieve rather than what function has to be performed.

There are some jobs which lend themselves easily to measured standards: a salesperson can be judged by the service given or the goods sold. But for others, such as research scientists, teachers, or solicitors, it is far harder to commit to paper an acceptable level of performance. However, it is always possible for the manager to outline acceptable and unacceptable methods or results. Setting standards ensures that this is clearly explained and understood.

People need to be able to monitor their own performance against such standards as well as expecting their own boss to periodically check results throughout the year.

There are six areas in which standards may be set:

- *numeric*—sales or production figures, defect levels, paper flow, visiting rates
- *deadlines*—completion of projects to time, turnaround of correspondence, statutory time limits, regularly meeting dates, answering phones, accounting deadlines
- *financial*—working to budgets on income and expenditure, meeting profit forecasts, stock levels, reduction in costs
- *procedural*—stages in writing a computer program, organisation liaison systems, timing on replies to customer complaints, giving information
- *negative*—number of complaints, feedback from colleagues, cancellations of work
- *recognisable*—corporate approach to customers, standards of dress, presentations to meetings, typing errors, house style.

Examples of standards of performance

A standard of performance is a continuing yardstick for judging when performance is at an acceptable level.

- Sales representative—call rate averages eight per day at an average of 18 miles per call.
- Social worker—in category 'A' cases, visiting takes place at least every four weeks and is followed by a full report to the supervisor.
- Plant manager—no more than two export orders per year fail to meet the shipping date.
- Office manager—all job applicants are acknowledged within two days and updated at intervals of not more than three weeks.
- Scientist—at least two research papers are produced each year.
- Teacher—meetings to consult and liaise with parents are set and attended.

6

SETTING TARGETS

Having established the requirements of the job, the next stage is to consider how targets can be used throughout the year as a normal part of the management process to enable staff to give their best performance.

Areas for target setting

Targets not only relate to sales or production figures, but also to results which cannot be as easily quantified. Therefore, providing both the boss and the job holder understand the tangible results which are expected, improving relations with another department can be as valid a target as reducing expenditure by 4 per cent.

Targets may therefore be set to:

- set a standard of performance
- raise a standard of performance
- re-establish slipping targets or standards
- progressively train job holder up to standard
- achieve a project often put aside
- innovate
- broaden individual skills
- develop the individual
- cash-in on unforseen circumstances
- implement a new policy
- develop a new area of work
- change priorities due to altered circumstances
- direct the high achiever.

How are targets set?

The manager has now discussed with the job holder what is expected from the job and what standards of performance must be maintained. Before setting targets, the manager should also look at available examples of what has been done—this will help in deciding what can be done.

Targets are set by the manager after consultation with the job holder. To avoid future argument about whether or not they have been achieved, targets should always be kept clear and simple, set at a face-to-face meeting, and recorded. People need to know what is required, when it is required and what priority it has in relation to other targets or routine work. The manager should not tell the job holder how to achieve the target but should allow scope for the job holder to exercise initiative.

Examples of targets

A target is a special task which needs to be achieved over and above the routine work.

- Sales representative—to gain three new accounts of at least £200 per calender month in 'x' month.
- Social worker—to establish regular liaison meetings with the local community policeman commencing . . .
- Office manager—to install a house style manual for departmental letters and forms by . . .
- Scientist—investigate availability of new instrumentation for 'x' and present the investment proposal to the Research Committee Meeting In . . . .
- Teacher—to take 'x' month on secondment with local industry and to produce a report for the Curriculum Committee on how the school can improve links with local businesses.

Clearly, every effort should be made to get the job holder to agree to the targets as this will make their commitment greater. In cases where this proves impossible, the manager must have the final say. Providing the job holder has been consulted and the reasons for setting the targets are clearly explained, it should be possible to get the job holder's acceptance. Appendix 1 gives a sample questionnaire which is intended to help this process.

How many?

If more than half-a-dozen targets are attempted in any one period, success in all of them is unlikely. People will not be able to concentrate on too many unless they are routine, in which case they lose their challenge. The number will reflect the difficulty and time span but it is not necessary to spread targets clinically over each result area. They should rather attack those areas where the need is greatest. Remember that targets are *special tasks over and above the routine areas* and, as performance standards have already been drawn up, other key result areas will not be neglected.

How precise?

Targets should be precise enough to avoid argument as to whether or not they have been achieved, but not so precise that they state the method by which the target is to be attempted as well as the goal itself. People need to know what is required, the deadline and what is the priority in relation to other targets or routine work, but the manager should allow scope for the job holder to exercise initiative in carrying out the relevant target.

For what period?

There is no ideal time limit for a target but if more than one or two targets have been set, it is wise to stagger the deadlines. Human nature determines that most people only complete a target close to deadline; if several all fall at once there will not be enough time for the job holder to concentrate on each and the quality of the results will suffer.

The time span for carrying out a target could be anything from a day to a year. However, if a job holder's enthusiasm is to be maintained, shorter time limits (one to six months) are better.

How difficult?

If targets are to improve performance and motivate people, there is no point in making them too easy. They should be challenging and stretching to develop a person and give them a real sense of achievement. They must also be realistic: what may be an easy target for an established employee may be too difficult for a new employee working through an induction period. Moreover, if the job holder does not think a target is realistic, commitment at the beginning is unlikely. This re-emphasises the need for the manager to get the job holder's views before setting a target. However, it could be that the manager will have to tone down an employee's enthusiasm and set an easier, more realistic target. Remember that whereas standards of performance relate to a job, targets relate to an individual and therefore should be more flexible.

How subject to change?

Flexibility is important as there is always a danger when setting targets that other factors may change their priority, rendering them irrelevant, too difficult, or too easy. Frequent monitoring will assist greatly. It is important also that targets are not dropped at the first sign of trouble as this rapidly discredits the whole concept and allows people to make excuses. The job of a manager when faced with a problem is to identify what other actions need to be taken to overcome it, rather than move the goal posts. Difficulties encountered in achieving targets should be viewed in this light.

How to monitor?

The likelihood of change and its effect on targets set means that the process must be monitored and, indeed, there is little point in setting a target unless there is some means for checking progress. The method for monitoring should be established when targets are set so that job holders are not taken by surprise or feel spied upon by a manager who has no faith in them.

Walking the job

Apart from regular systems for exchanging information such as monthly figures, reports and so on, a more informal method of checking on progress is 'walking the job': that is, simply going around the team and asking how they are getting on. This can also be a useful occasion to recognise progress and proffer informal advice if needed.

One-to-one meetings

However, it is important that meetings for reviewing due targets, considering progress on others and setting new ones are arranged regularly. This will ensure that target setting becomes part of the management process and that targets and progress are considered throughout the year and adapted to the needs of the organisation, department and job holder. It will also give job holders a regular opportunity to discuss their work away from the hurly-burly of daily pressures, and shift the balance of work away from 'fire-fighting' to looking ahead.

Ideally, review meetings should take place monthly and certainly no less than quarterly. They should be short with only a brief confirmation of progress and action, and should include the following points:

- have the targets been achieved and if so what can be learned from them?
- if any targets have not been achieved is this due to:
  —failure on the job holder's part such as leaving it too late
  —the manager's failure such as providing insufficient resources or authority
  —unforseen circumstances, for example absence through sickness or extra workload?
- if the target has not been met, should the deadline be extended, alternative methods adopted or has the target been rendered irrelevant?
- how is the individual doing in relation to the routine areas of their job?

It is important for the manager to be constructive at these reviews. Successes and failures should be identified and new targets and positive action set. It should not be seen as a chance for the manager or job holder to apportion blame. The emphasis should be on assessing people on what they have achieved rather than on abstract personal qualities.

Records

Target setting is about dialogue and commitment to action rather than paperwork. However, it is important to keep a record if only by means of a memo confirming progress and new targets. A more structured approach will assist, particularly where people are not used to the concept and there is a need to provide information upwards to the boss's boss or to identify training needs. A full scale appraisal should be carried out at least once per year. Appendices 2, 3 and 4 provide examples of an appraisal policy, a counselling questionnaire, and a review form, respectively.

7

SUMMARY

Essentially, target setting is a simple and obvious procedure which helps individuals to develop and an organisation to be more successful. However, it should not be seen as a panacea which will transform things overnight. Some jobs and cultures lend themselves better to target setting than others. What is certain is that unless people are clear about what is expected of them and the direction they are taking, and unless they regularly talk things through with their boss, the organisation will miss out on a very effective method of tapping talent, gaining commitment and improving results.

Target setting may be put into effect by any manager whether or not a formal appraisal scheme exists. If one does then the regular target reviews will form the backbone of the scheme—the annual appraisal being the strategic review, and the regular reviews providing information during the year to help give an accurate record of performance and to provide the dynamic forward-looking part of the scheme.

The main benefits of setting targets are those directly related to getting a task done and motivating the individual. However, there are supplementary benefits such as helping to identify training needs, or identifying potential. The latter is a very complicated subject of which progress against targets is only one part. It does provide a record of achievement and therefore helps to reduce subjectivity and, if based upon suitable targets, can indicate how an individual will tackle a challenge in an area of little experience.

II

APPENDICES

APPENDIX 1

TARGET ANALYSIS QUESTIONNAIRE

When setting targets it is essential that the following questions are asked.

1 How significant is this target in terms of the known objectives of this organisation?
2 How urgent is this target?
3 To what extent is this target measurable? (Consider the yardsticks you have developed.)
4 How clearly is this target described? Does it precisely describe the end results expected?
5 What should the target completion date be? To what extent does this target statement describe an activity leading to a target as opposed to a real end result?
6 To what extent is this target challenging as opposed to being routine? That is, to what extent does this target stretch the individual?

APPENDIX 2

PERFORMANCE APPRAISAL

A minimal organisation policy.

1 All employees shall have a discussion at least once a year with their manager about their performance. The discussion should recognise good performance and address weaker areas. Most of the content should relate to the future and should result in a specific plan for targets, training, and development to help the individual improve.

2 The immediate line manager is responsible for seeing that this is done.

3 The discussion shall take place AT LEAST once a year.

4 Both parties should prepare for the interview and have an input on previous performance and priorities for the future.

5 The conclusions of the manager AFTER the interview shall be written on the appropriate form and individuals shall have the opportunity to add written comments if they wish.

6 Either during the interview, or soon after, a limited number of important targets shall be set on areas of work where progress is needed during the coming period. The person accountable, the timescale and result required should be clearly indicated.

7 Performance against these targets and key result areas should be reviewed regularly throughout the year.

APPENDIX 3

COUNSELLING AND APPRAISAL

Questions for the job holder.

1 Consider your performance in your present job. What have you accomplished and how efficiently was it done?
What difficulties did you encounter?

2 What do you consider to be the most important responsibilities of your present job?

3 Do you feel that your present job fully utilises your abilities, training and interests? If not, which of your abilities could be utilised?
How would your job have to be changed to accomplish this?

4 What aspect of the job interests you:
(a) the most?
(b) the least?

5 Do you feel there are some areas of difficulty in your job performance? If so, what action do you feel might be taken to overcome these by yourself or your manager?

6 What kind of work would you like to be doing two to five years from now?

7 Would any special training or experience be required for you to do such work?

APPENDIX 4

TARGETS AND PERFORMANCE REVIEW FORM

1 Name of job holder

2 Department

3 Title of job

4 Date of commencing job

5 Name of immediate boss

6 Name of boss's boss

7 Date when targets were set

8 Date of revisions, if any

9 Date of performance review

10 Dates of intermediate reviews, if any

11 Proposals, if any, for improving contribution by training, extra experience or promotion

12 Comments by job holder on performance review (18 & 19)

Signed ....

Date ....

13 Date of last performance review form

Do comments still stand?

14 Comments in 12 noted

Signature of boss ....

Date ....

15 Comments by boss's boss and proposed action in 11 noted

Signed ....

Date ....

16 Objectives of job

17 Main points job holder should concentrate on

1 _____

2 _____

3 _____

4 _____

5 _____

6 _____

7 _____

18 Performance review

1 _____

2 _____

3 _____

4 _____

5 _____

6 _____

7 _____

19 Other comments on performance

Notes: 1 Ask people for whom you (the boss) are responsible for their suggested targets
2 Discuss with them, set targets, and fill in **16** and **17** and complete **1–7**
3 If targets revised, note in **8**
4 At date of review, complete **9**, **10**, **11**, **18** and **19**
5 Discuss reviews with people concerned. They should complete **12**
6 Complete **13** and **14**
7 Pass to boss's boss to complete **15**, and return to boss of job holder

• The form can be simplified through the deletion of steps **8**, and **10–16**.